CITY ATLAS

TRAVEL THE WORLD WITH 30 CITY MAPS

WIDE EYED EDITIONS

contents

34. Moscow

44. San Francisco

54. Hong Kong

36. Montreal

46. Mexico City

56. Tokyo

38. Toronto

48. Rio de Janeiro

58. Seoul

40. Chicago

50. Buenos Aires

60. Mumbai

42. New York

52. Cape Town

62. Sydney

LISBON

Famous for its custard tarts, Lisbon is the vibrant capital of Portugal. Spread over seven low hills, this beautiful city is even older than Rome. Ride on its vintage yellow trams, visit its many churches, and learn to surf on the nearby beaches.

Can you find **5** COCKERELS?

Country: PORTUGAL
Language: PORTUGUESE
Population: 0.55 MILLION

Find yourself in an enchanted forest at JARDIM ZOOLÓGICO

Find a giant falcon in the galleries of the CALOUSTE GULBENKIAN COLLECTION

Stumble across a hidden statue in the gardens of ESTUFA FRIA

Take some time out in a teepee at the ALTO DA SERAFINA ADVENTURE PLAYGROUND

Go crazy for Portuguese CUSTARD TARTS

Pop in to see the Portuguese Parliament at PALÁCIO DE SÃO BENTO

Learn to surf on the CASCAIS BEACHES

Enjoy a peaceful pause in the BASILICA DA ESTRELA

See the ships come sailing in at DOCA DE ALCÂNTARA

Be swept away by the naval museum, MUSEU DE MARINHA

RIVER TAGUS

Take a tour of the CAMPO PEQUENO BULLRING

Catch a concert at PARQUE DA BELA VISTA

Cross the Vasco da Gama Bridge—the longest in Europe!

Sleep with the fishes at the OCEANARIUM

Go green in the gardens of ALAMEDA DOM AFONSO HENRIQUES

See some super-sized street art in the SALDANHA NEIGHBORHOOD

Interact with science and technology in the Pavilion of Knowledge at CIÊNCIA VIVA

Hitch a ride on the funicular, ELEVADOR DA GLÓRIA

Take a picture of the TILED HOUSES

Get a 360-degree view from the dome of the NATIONAL PANTHEON OF SANTA ENGRÁCIA

Olá

Storm the battlements of the Moorish CASTLE OF SÃO JORGE

Wander around the PRAÇA DO COMÉRCIO

Be drawn in by contemporary art at the MUSEU DO CHIADO

Hop on a ferry across the RIVER TAGUS

Indulge in some CHURROS AND HOT CHOCOLATE

Run wild in Gaudí's outdoor world of wonder, PARK GÜELL

Take a tour of architect Antoni Gaudí's masterpiece, CASA BATLLÓ

Climb the Nativity tower at SAGRADA FAMÍLIA

Make magic and mischief at TEATRE MUSEU EL REI DE LA MÀGIA

Fall in love with FLAMENCO—a traditional Spanish style of dance

Make your way to MACBA, Barcelona's Museum of Contemporary Art!

See the street performers on LA RAMBLA

See some of Miró's masterpieces in PARC DE JOAN MIRÓ

Work up your appetite for a PAELLA PARTY!

Sleep away the afternoon with a SPANISH SIESTA

Take a tour of the famous CAMP NOU STADIUM—home of the famous Barcelona soccer team

Make friends with THE RAVAL CAT—a sculpture by Fernando Botero

SHIPS AHOY! Watch the boats come in to dock

See the spectacular performance of the MAGIC FOUNTAIN OF MONTJUIC

Catch a cable car to MONTJUIC CASTLE

BARCELONA

This city on the sea is the second largest in Spain, and the capital of the autonomous community of Catalonia. Barcelona's warm climate lends itself to a slower pace of life, so kick back and enjoy a lunchtime "siesta" nap! Look out for the friendly Raval Cat, try out the tasty tapas, and wander around Gaudí's wonderfully weird La Sagrada Familia cathedral.

Can you find **5** RED BULLS

Country: SPAIN
Language: SPANISH
Population: 1.6 MILLION

March to victory under the ARC DE TRIOMF

Visit Barcelona's zoo in the PARC de la CIUTADELLA

Pick out your favorite painting at the MUSEU PICASSO

Go gothic at the CATEDRAL DE BARCELONA

Spot the sculpture of a GIANT GOLDFISH by Frank Gehry

Discover Barri Gòtic's backstreet tabernas and tuck into some TASTY TAPAS!

Eat an ice cream on the PALM TREE PROMENADE

Spend a day in the sun at the BEACH

Spend a star-studded night at the open-air CINEMA LLIURE

MEDITERRANEAN SEA

London

The English capital is well known for its winding streets and big red buses—jump on board to see what's happening in this bustling city! Navigate the cultural maze, run wild in London Zoo, or escape the action on Regent's Canal.

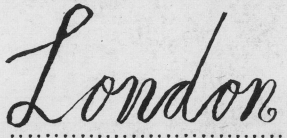

Can you find **5** RED BUSES?

Country: ENGLAND
Language: ENGLISH
Population: 8.3 MILLION

Explore REGENT'S CANAL with a waterway tour

Meet the penguins at LONDON ZOO

Do a King-sized Kickflip at BAY SIXTY6 SKATE PARK

See Sherlock Holmes's study at 221B BAKER STREET

Shop till you drop on OXFORD STREET

Haggle a deal at PORTOBELLO MARKET

Play pirates at the DIANA MEMORIAL PLAYGROUND

Rent pedalos on THE SERPENTINE

Count the hour with BIG BEN

Sleep over on Science Night at the SCIENCE MUSEUM

Watch the Changing of the Guard at BUCKINGHAM PALACE

Go wild at KEW GARDENS

Visit the dinosaurs at the NATURAL HISTORY MUSEUM

£1

Visit Platform 9¾ in KING'S CROSS STATION

Make a splash at LONDON FIELDS LIDO

hello

Eat fish and chips at BROADWAY MARKET

Discover a mummy at THE BRITISH MUSEUM

Play telephone at ST. PAUL'S Whispering Gallery

Buy a bunch of flowers at COLUMBIA ROAD FLOWER MARKET

Explore the V&A MUSEUM OF CHILDHOOD

CLERKENWELL ROAD

See some street art on BRICK LANE

Discover a tropical oasis in the BARBICAN CENTRE'S rooftop conservatory

Visit SPITALFIELDS, one of London's oldest markets

Spot a famous face at the NATIONAL PORTRAIT GALLERY

Join the crowd at SHAKESPEARE'S GLOBE

Watch TOWER BRIDGE light up at night

RIVER THAMES

Be a culture vulture on the SOUTH BANK

Go for a spin on the LONDON EYE

See the sights from a DOUBLE-DECKER BUS

AMSTERDAM

Amsterdam is the capital of the Kingdom of the Netherlands and is built around sixty miles of interconnecting canals. There are more bikes here than permanent residents, and more museums per square foot than any other city—so pop on your helmet and take a tour!

Can you find **5** CANAL BOATS

Country: NETHERLANDS
Language: DUTCH
Population: 0.8 MILLION

Learn about the Netherlands's unofficial national flower at the AMSTERDAM TULIP MUSEUM

See Anne Frank's secret annex during World War II at the ANNE FRANK HUIS

Live like a king at the ROYAL PALACE AND GARDENS

Explore the waterways with a CANAL CRUISE

Savor a slice of DUTCH PEACH PIE

Find your favorite flower at the fragrant BLOEMENMARKT

Be amazed by the incredible feats of Amsterdam's youth-based CIRCUS ELLEBOOG

Check out the children's program at the youth theater, JEUGDTHEATER DE KRAKELING

Travel through the city on a blue-and-white TRAM

Flip your own pancakes at the KINDERKOOKKAFÉ

Visit the VAN GOGH MUSEUM

Meet the Square Man at the RIJKSMUSEUM

Take time to unwind in the VONDELPARK

Catch a classical concert for free at CONCERTGEBOUW

Frolic in the fountains in front of the RIJKSMUSEUM

Visit the **CAT BOAT**, an alley cat sanctuary

Do some train spotting at **AMSTERDAM CENTRAAL STATION**

Discover the secret church in the MUSEUM **ONS' LIEVE HEER OP SOLDER**

Discover the Dutch Golden Age at the **REMBRANDT HOUSE MUSEUM**

RENT A BIKE and explore the city

IJHAVEN

Investigate alien life-forms at the **SCIENCE CENTER NEMO**

NEMO

Hallo

Draw the animals at the **ARTIS ROYAL ZOO**

See the giant lily pads at the **HORTUS BOTANICUS** botanical garden

Join a children's workshop at the **HERMITAGE AMSTERDAM MUSEUM**

AMSTEL RIVER

Cross the **MAGERE BRUG** or Skinny Bridge, over the **AMSTEL RIVER**

Play hide-and-seek at the **OOSTERPARK**

Try some famous **DUTCH CHEESES**: Edam, Gouda, and Leyden

11

Explore Parc monceau

Do a victory dance at the ARC DE TRIOMPHE

Join a guided bike tour

Sail boats at the TUILERIES FOUNTAINS

Salut

Catch the street performers on the CHAMPS-ÉLYSÉES

Gawk at the GRAND PALAIS'S glass roof

Wander in the woods of BOIS DE BOULOGNE

Buy a baguette at a BOULANGERIE

RIVER SEINE

Enter an underwater world at the AQUARIUM

Get arty at the MUSÉE D'ORSAY

Climb the EIFFEL TOWER

Visit NAPOLEON'S TOMB

Paris

Also known as the City of Light, the French capital is famous for its culture, cathedrals, and exquisite cuisine. Fall in love with everything in this romantic city and go for the Gallic specialties—frogs's legs and snails, anyone?

Can you find 5 FRENCH CHEESES?

Country: FRANCE
Language: FRENCH
Population: 2.3 MILLION

Search for spooks in Paris's CATACOMBS

Go glam at the
OPÉRA DE PARIS

Catch a performance
at the OPÉRA COMIQUE

Explore the PALAIS ROYAL GARDENS

ANGELINA

Try snails at
BRASSERIE FLO

Pack a picnic for
CANAL SAINT-MARTIN

Rent a bike at
13 RUE BRANTÔME

Check out the children's
gallery at the CENTRE POMPIDOU

Prowl through the
MUSÉE DE LA CHASSE
ET DE LA NATURE,
Museum of Hunting
and Nature

Meet Mona Lisa
at the LOUVRE

Bask on the beaches of the
SAND PLAGES in summer

Visit the
flower market
on ÎLE DE LA
CITÉ

Step back in time at
MUSÉE CARNAVALET

Wander the cobbled streets of
SAINT-GERMAIN-DES-PRÉS

Visit the home
of Quasimodo,
NOTRE DAME

Pick up a trick
at the
MUSEUM OF
MAGIC

Catch a puppet
show at the JARDIN
DU LUXEMBOURG

Shop for goodies on the
RUE MOUFFETARD

Go wild in the
MENAGERIE DU
JARDIN DES PLANTES

13

Go to Gladiator School with the HISTORIC GROUP OF ROME

Get interactive at EXPLORA, children's museum of science and history

Pop over to the "people's square", PIAZZA DEL POPOLO

Visit the VATICAN, the city in a city, and home of the Pope

Stare at the ceiling of the SISTINE CHAPEL

Hang out at HADRIAN'S TOMB, CASTEL SANT'ANGELO

Enjoy a busking bonanza in PIAZZA NAVONA

Marvel at PALAZZO BRASCHI'S mosaics

Take a trip back in time at the PANTHEON

RIVER TIBER

Be inspired by the inventions at MACCHINE DI LEONARDO DA VINCI

Get a table on TIBER ISLAND

ROME

People have lived in Rome for over two and half thousand years, which is perhaps the reason it is sometimes called the Eternal City! This is a great place to explore ancient ruins, learn about gory gladiators, and eat every flavor of the Italian ice cream speciality, gelato. When in Rome...!

Ciao

Can you find **5** SLICES OF PIZZA

Country: ITALY
Language: ITALIAN
Population: 2.7 MILLION

Pick up a roman-style PIZZA

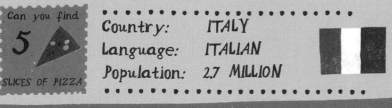

Take some snaps at the BIOPARCO DI ROMA—the zoological gardens

Escape the city at the VILLA BORGHESE

Pedal yourself around the park

Sit on the SPANISH STEPS at Piazza di Spagna

Toss a coin in the TREVI FOUNTAIN

Explore ancient ruins at the ROMAN FORUM

Pay a visit to Rome's Flavian Amphitheatre, the COLOSSEUM

See the excavations at SAN CLEMENTE

Check out CIRCUS MAXIMUS, the home of chariot racing

Explore VILLA CELIMONTANA'S abandoned ancient temples

Gorge on GELATO— delicious Italian ice cream

Best pizza in Rome? Grab a slice at SFORNO!

Berlin

Berlin is the vibrant capital of Germany, where the world-famous physicist Albert Einstein lived between 1914 and 1932. Explore the city's many museums and memorials, eat your weight in gummy bears, and head for the historical highlights, including Checkpoint Charlie, where the Berlin Wall once stood.

Can you find **5** DOUGHNUTS?

Country: GERMANY
Language: GERMAN
Population: 3.5 MILLION

Rent canoes on the WATERWAYS

Hallo

Head down to FRITZ-SCHLOSS PARK

Get going at the BERLIN CENTRAL STATION, or BERLIN HAUPTBAHNHOF

Sightsee from the NO. 100 BUS

See the city skyline from the REICHSTAG BUILDING

Go through the BRANDENBURG GATE

Visit the HOLOCAUST MEMORIAL

Roam around the TIERGARTEN

Block out some time for LEGOLAND

Enter through the Elephant Gates at ZOO BERLIN

Get a prickly welcome at the BERLIN-DAHLEM BOTANICAL GARDEN

Let your ideas take flight at the GERMAN MUSEUM OF TECHNOLOGY

Clown around at JUXIRKUS, Berlin's oldest youth circus

Explore Berlin's underworld with an UNTERWELTEN tour

Experience gummy bear paradise, BÄRENLAND

Find out Berlin's famous fast food, CURRYWURST

Get hands-on at Kids' museum MACHMit! MUSEUM FOR CHILDREN

Make your way to the BERLIN WALL MEMORIAL

ERICH
ACHTUNG SNAKE
YOU
ROB
ICH LIEBE DICH

Discover a dinosaur at the MUSEUM FÜR NATURKUNDE

Meet the EAST BERLIN AMPELMANN

Friedrichstadt Palast

Meet the Egyptian pharaoh Nefertiti at the NEUES MUSEUM

RIVER SPREE

Buy a bratwurst in ALEXANDERPLATZ

Go to the BERLIN TV TOWER and eat in a revolving restaurant

Be blown away by BERLIN CATHEDRAL

See the seat of the mayor at RED CITY HALL, or ROTES RATHAUS

Listen out for the bells of the FRENCH CHURCH OF FRIEDRICHSTADT

Check out CHECKPOINT CHARLIE

Take time to look around the JEWISH MUSEUM

ICH BIN EIN BERLINER

Get crafty at the children's art workshop, LA BASTELLERIE

Get your skates on at
KALLION KENTTÄ ICE RINK

Catch a show
at the CIRKO
CENTER FOR
NEW CIRCUS

Glory in the
grandeur of
HELSINKI CATHEDRAL

Get a boost at the
KAISANIEMI BOTANIC
GARDEN

See what's on display at
ATENEUM ART MUSEUM

Brave the BIG
CAT VALLEY at
Helsinki Zoo

Step inside the
USPENSKI CATHEDRAL

Rent bikes to see the
city sights

Catch a ferry at
HELSINKI PORT

See the latest
show at the
DESIGN MUSEUM

Kick back at
KAIVOPUISTO PARK

Go green at HARAKKA
NATURE CENTER

Helsinki

The capital of Finland, Helsinki, is a seaside city—head to
the harbor and catch a ferry to explore the surrounding
bays, inlets, and small islands. Visit in the spring when the
sun comes out and you'll see the city come to life with people
exploring its green spaces and beautiful buildings.

Can you find
5
REINDEER

Country: FINLAND
Language: FINNISH
Population: 0.62 MILLION

Take a refreshing dip in the FROGNERBADET outdoor pools

Play princes and princesses at the ROYAL PALACE

Tap your feet by the bandstand of ST. HANSHAUGEN PARK

Scout out the sculptures in the VIGELAND PARK

Get cultural at the NATIONAL MUSEUM OF ART, ARCHITECTURE, AND DESIGN

Savor a super-fresh NORWEGIAN SALMON

Relive past times at the NORWEGIAN MUSEUM OF CULTURAL HISTORY

Learn about past prizewinners at the NOBEL PEACE CENTER

Find a modern masterpiece at the ASTRUP FEARNLEY MUSEUM

Catch a show at the NATIONAL THEATER

Visit the longship at the VIKING SHIP MUSEUM

Set sail from the OSLO HARBOR

See the fjords from the AKERSHUS FORTRESS

Cycle the trail around the BYGDØY PENINSULA

Go fishing in the OSLOFJORD!

Take a dip off the island HOVEDØYA

INNER OSLOFJORD

Kick back in KUBA PARK

Meet IDA, the oldest primate fossil in the world!

Hallo

Hear the bells toll outside the OSLO DOMKIRKE

Pack your goggles for the TOYENBADET SWIMMING POOL

Try a tasty CINNAMON BUN

Tip your hat to the tiger outside OSLO CENTRAL STATION

Get your mouth around the traditional Norwegian dessert, MULTEKREM, with cloudberries

Watch a ballet at the OPERAHUSET, Oslo's opera house

Try your hand at PADDLEBOARDING

OSLO

Norway's capital Oslo is also known as the "Land of the Midnight Sun" because of its long days in summer. Get outside in this active city: learn to ski, get your skates on, or go fishing in the Oslofjord... Whichever you choose, be sure to warm up with a hot chocolate and cinnamon bun afterward!

Can you find 5 VIKINGS?

Country: NORWAY
Language: NORWEGIAN
Population: 0.63 MILLION

Copenhagen

Denmark has been voted the happiest country in the world, and Copenhagen is its cool capital. Famous for its lakes, this exciting cultural center also boasts the world's second-oldest amusement park, Tivoli Gardens. Make time to find your favorite Danish pastry and meet the Little Mermaid.

Can you find **5** CYCLISTS?

Country: DENMARK
Language: DANISH
Population: 1.2 MILLION

Go for a paddle at the FÆLLEDPARKEN WATER PARK

Try your tricks out at the FÆLLEDPARKEN SKATEPARK

Hej

Pick your perfect painting at STATENS MUSEUM FOR KUNST

Feed the ducks on one of the LAKES

Be sure to see the beautiful BOTANICAL GARDENS

Become acquainted with Copenhagen's famous astronomer TYCHO BRAHE

Try some Danish delicacies at the TORVEHALLERNE MARKET

Stalk the STORK FOUNTAIN!

Go star gazing at the TYCHO BRAHE PLANETARIUM

Be wowed by the world clock in COPENHAGEN CITY HALL

See the seat of the Danish Parliament CHRISTIANSBORG PALACE

Check out the CHILDREN'S MUSEUM

Take a picture of a polar bear at COPENHAGEN ZOO

Ride the roller coaster at the TIVOLI GARDENS

Take the plunge at the outdoor HARBOR BATHS

Decide on your favorite DANISH PASTRY

Meet the LITTLE MERMAID

ØRESUND

Explore the star-shaped KASTELLET sea fortress

Drop by the display of decorative arts and crafts at the DANISH MUSEUM OF ART AND DESIGN

Tuck into a SMØRREBRØD— an open sandwich

Revel in Rococo architecture at AMALIENBORG PALACE

Marvel at the "Marble Church," FREDERIK'S CHURCH

Hit a high note at COPENHAGEN OPERA HOUSE

Dig for fossils at the science center, EXPERIMENTARIUM CITY

Drop by "THE BLACK DIAMOND," the Royal Library

Play at being pirates on the AMAGER BEACH PARK

Explore the amazing BLUE PLANET AQUARIUM

Climb the golden spire of the CHURCH OF OUR SAVIOUR

Stockholm

The environmentally-friendly city of Stockholm is the capital of Sweden and is spread over fourteen islands. Between the years 800–1100, its lands were home to the master sailors, the Vikings, and the city has had a rich nautical history ever since—learn all about this at the Vasa Museum.

Can you find **5** CROWNS?

Country: SWEDEN
Language: SWEDISH
Population: 0.9 MILLION

Be amazed by the art in the STOCKHOLM METRO STATIONS

Try some Swedish sweets, called "GODIS"

See the crown jewels at the ROYAL PALACE

Watch a production at the eighteenth-century theater of DROTTNINGHOLM PALACE

Feel like a dignitary as you descend the staircase in STOCKHOLM CITY HALL

Walk the Nobel Prize Hall of Fame at the NOBELMUSEET

RIDDARFJÄRDEN

Hellå

Explore GAMLA STAN, Stockholm's medieval Old Town

Go for a dip at the LÅNGHOLM ROCKS and BEACH

Pick up a PICKLED GHERKIN or two!

Splash down at
KAMPEMENTSBADET
OUTDOOR SWIMMING POOL

Learn about longships
on a VIKING HISTORY
TOUR

Monkey around
in GÄRDET ROYAL
PARK

Munch on a
SWEDISH MEATBALL

Enjoy a Night at the Museum and explore
the NATIONAL MUSEUM OF SCIENCE AND
TECHNOLOGY, or TEKNISKA MUSEET

DJURGÅRDSBRUNNSVIKEN

Meet Pippi Longstocking
at STORYBOOK SQUARE
in Junibacken

Visit SKANSEN,
the world's first
open-air museum

Visit the ROSENDAL
BOTANICAL GARDENS, or
ROSENDALS TRÄDGÅRD

Run wild
in the ROYAL
DJURGÅRDEN

See the mysterious 17th-
century ghost ship at the
VASAMUSEET

Have an adventure in
the rain forest of
AQUARIA VATTENMUSEUM

Celebrate the spring festival
of WALPURGISNACHT—the
Night of the Witches

Get arty at the
MODERNA MUSEET

Be a Dancing Queen
at the ABBA MUSEUM

Have a magical day
at GRÖNA LUND
AMUSEMENT PARK

Make some furry
friends at the
PETTING ZOO

WALDEMARSVIKEN

Explore the islands
on A BOAT TRIP

Float above the city
in a glass bubble with
STOCKHOLM SKYVIEW

Try some tasty
FRIED HERRING

Athens

Athens is the capital of Greece and it's one of the oldest cities in the world—often described as the birthplace of Western civilization. It's a great place to explore ancient ruins and learn about Greek gods, but be sure to try the delicious and colorful Greek salads, and brilliant, sweet baklavas too.

Can you find 5 GOLD MEDALS?

Country: GREECE
Language: GREEK
Population: 0.7 MILLION

Make your way to the HELLENIC MOTOR MUSEUM

The famous philosophers SOCRATES AND ARISTOTLE both lived in ancient Athens

Be taken for a roller coaster ride at ALLOU! FUN PARK

Time-travel to ancient Greece with the FOUNDATION OF THE HELLENIC WORLD

Be dazzled by the beautiful BENAKI MUSEUM of Islamic art

Watch a show at the HARIDIMOS SHADOW PUPPET MUSEUM

Take in the city lights with an ATHENS NIGHT WALKING TOUR

Explore the ancient citadel, the ACROPOLIS OF ATHENS

Explore the neighborhood of ANAFIOTIKA

Meet the Greek gods at the ACROPOLIS MUSEUM

Climb up FILOPAPPOU HILL, the Hill of the Muses

Try some tasty MOUSSAKA at a traditional taverna

ARES, the ancient Greek god of war

Take a class in GREEK COOKING

Unearth a discovery at the NATIONAL ARCHAEOLOGICAL MUSEUM

Ride a cable car to the top of MOUNT LYCABETTUS

Meet the animals at ATTICA ZOOLOGICAL PARK

Find inspiration in the NATIONAL ART GALLERY

Γεια σας

See the Changing of the Guard outside the GREEK PARLIAMENT

See the hand-crafted costumes at the Greek Folk Art Museum

Spend a day at the NATIONAL GARDEN

Go through Hadrian's Gate, THE ARCH OF HADRIAN

Get an idea of ancient Greece's grandeur at the TEMPLE OF ZEUS

ATHENA, the ancient Greek goddess of war

POSEIDON, the ancient Greek god of the sea

HERMES, the messenger of the ancient Greek gods

ZEUS, the King of the ancient Greek gods

See planes, trains, and automobiles at the RAHMI M. KOÇ MUSEUM, and get starry-eyed at DISCOVERY SPHERE PLANETARIUM

See the spectacular GOLDEN HORN at sunset

Tuck into some tasty TURKISH KEBABS

Climb the gigantic GALATA TOWER

Galata Bridge

Istanbul

This city was first built in Byzantine times, more than 2,600 years ago! Chat with the friendly locals, bask on the brilliant beaches, and hop on board a boat tour to get the best view of the beautiful Bosphorus.

Can you find 5 BLUE EVIL EYES?

Country: TURKEY
Language: TURKISH
Population: 3 MILLION

Look out for lamps at the GRAND BAZAAR

Have an adventure at

See the EGYPTIAN OBELISK of Pharaoh Thutmose III

Stroll through the serene
ATATURK ARBORETUM

See the sights
at TAKSIM SQUARE

Travel back in
time on a tram at
ISTIKLÂL CADDESI

Take a boat tour
on the BOSPHORUS
STRAIT

Merhaba

BOSPHORUS
STRAIT

ISTANBUL MODERN

Spot a masterpiece at
the ISTANBUL MUSEUM OF
MODERN ART

Get Istan-cool at
ISTANBUL'74 arts festival

Take a trip out to
KIZ KULESI,
THE MAIDEN'S TOWER

Catch a ferry
to ADALAR, the
Princes' Islands

Find ancient artifacts
at the ISTANBUL
ARCHAEOLOGICAL MUSEUMS

Spend the day sultan-style at the
TOPKAPI PALACE AND GARDENS

Explore outdoors at
GÜLHANE PARK

HAGIA SOPHIA MUSEUM

Make a wish at
the BASILICA CISTERN

Marvel at the stupendous
SULTAN AHMED MOSQUE, or
BLUE MOSQUE

Wave at the animals as you fly overhead
on the chairlift at ZOO PRAHA

Climb the Great
South Tower at
ST. VITUS CATHEDRAL

Jump aboard the
HISTORIC TRAM 91 for
a ride around the city

Catch a puppet
show at the
NATIONAL
MARIONETTE
THEATER

Count the statues
on CHARLES BRIDGE

Rent roller skates
near PRAGUE CASTLE

Climb 300 steps to the
top of the PETŘÍN
OBSERVATION TOWER

Ride the Funicular
Railway to the top
of PETŘÍN HILL

VLTAVA RIVER

Discover KRANNER'S
FOUNTAIN in the heart
of the Old Town

Feed the ducks
on PETŘÍN POND

Indulge in some KOLÁČ,
a kind of CZECH CAKE

Ahoj

Take a boat ride
along the VLTAVA
RIVER and enjoy a
day on the water

Visit Fred and Ginger—
THE DANCING HOUSE

Fly a kite in LETNÁ PARK

Prague

This is the romantic capital of the Czech Republic. During the Renaissance of the 14th to the 17th centuries, it was a major European city, and some amazing castles, bridges, and cathedrals were built. Climb the St Vitus Cathedral, count the statues on Charles Bridge, and see the world's oldest working astronomical clock.

Can you find **5** DANCING GIRLS?

Country: CZECH REPUBLIC
Language: CZECH
Population: 1.2 MILLION

Count the gargoyles in STARÉ MĚSTO

Tell the time by the world-famous ASTRONOMICAL CLOCK

Join a GHOSTS AND LEGENDS walking tour

Find out about the city's history at the MUSEUM OF THE CITY OF PRAGUE

Go straight to the top of the ŽIŽKOV TV TOWER

Catch a train at PRAGUE STATION

Watch a mime artist at the BLACK LIGHT THEATER

Wander through WENCESLAS SQUARE

Catch the local symphony playing in the lobby of the NATIONAL MUSEUM

Marvel at the Neo-Gothic CHURCH OF ST. LUDMILA

See the city streets from the ELIZABETH LOOKOUT tower

Bask in the park on MARGARET ISLAND

Glide over the treetops on the LIBEGŐ chairlift

Catch a CHOCOLATE CHRISTMAS CONCERT for children

Wander along the blue DANUBE

Explore the MILLENÁRIS Playground and Exhibition Park

Ride the Budapest COG-WHEEL RAILWAY

Have an adventure in the BUDA HILLS

Visit the Fisherman's Bastion

Check out the spectacular SZÉCHENYI CHAIN BRIDGE

Treat yourself to some warm APPLE STRUDEL

Cast your eye on BUDA CASTLE

Zip about at the CHALLENGELAND treetop playground

Discover the city's past at the BUDAPEST HISTORY MUSEUM

Gorge on Budapest's gourmet GOULASH

Budapest

Budapest is the magical capital of Hungary. It became a single city in 1873 when Buda and Óbuda, on the west bank of the great River Danube, were unified with Pest, on the east bank. Have an adventure in the Buda Hills, make a splash in the famous thermal baths, and be amazed by all of the beautiful buildings in between!

Can you find

5

BOWLS OF GOULASH?

Country: HUNGARY
Language: HUNGARIAN
Population: 1.7 MILLION

Climb up Gellért Hill to the CITADEL FORTRESS

Discover the fabulous flora and fauna at BUDAPEST ZOO AND BOTANICAL GARDEN

Warm your heart at the SZÉCHENYI THERMAL BATH

Get a move on at BUDAPEST-NYUGATI RAILWAY TERMINAL

Get your skates on at the CITY PARK ICE RINK

See planes, trains, and automobiles at the TRANSPORT MUSEUM

See the domes on the Danube at the HUNGARIAN PARLIAMENT BUILDING

Szia

Spot the ancient district boundaries by the OLD CITY WALLS

Learn about STEPHEN I, the first King of Hungary

See the panoramic view of the ST. STEPHEN'S BASILICA

Take a guided tour through the MUSEUM OF APPLIED ARTS

RIVER DANUBE

Try a creamy, cheesy sajtos roló PASTRY

Shop till you drop at the BUDAPEST WHALE

Listen out for the musical activities at Budapest's PALACE OF ARTS

Learn about the universe at the PLANETÁRIUM

MOSCOW

Moscow, capital of Russia, is named after the Moskva River, which runs through the city. It is home to the extravagant St. Basil's Cathedral, which was built by Ivan the Terrible in the 16th century. There is a lot to see and explore in this fantastic city, but wrap up warm in winter—temperatures here can average 14°F!

Can you find **5** RUSSIAN DOLLS?

Country: RUSSIA
Language: RUSSIAN
Population: 12 MILLION

Explore the interactive science museum EXPERIMENTARIUM

Go ice-skating ALL-RUSSIAN EXHIBITION CENTER

Learn about the emperor PETER THE GREAT, who was born in Moscow in 1672

Visit the magnificent MAYAKOVSKAYA METRO STATION

Meet the bears at MOSCOW ZOO

Enjoy some authentic RUSSIAN COOKING

Take a tour on the magnificent MOSCOW METRO

Explore the colorful ALEXANDER GARDENS

MOSKVA RIVER

Catch a performance of Peter and the Wolf at NATALIA SATS CHILDREN'S MUSICAL THEATER

Gawk at the golden domes of the CATHEDRAL OF CHRIST THE SAVIOUR

Ride the Ferris wheel at the GORKY AMUSEMENT PARK

Get a taste of Star
City at the MUSEUM
OF COSMONAUTICS

Привет
(Privet)

Watch the Russian
Ballet at the famous
BOLSHOI THEATER

RED SQUARE

Discover the KREMLIN,
a fortress in a city

Be inspired by
the ornate onion domes of
ST. BASIL'S CATHEDRAL

Be amazed by the
MOSCOW STATE
CIRCUS

Visit the ZKP TAGANSKY
COLD WAR MUSEUM

Explore the
city with a
walking tour

Go cuckoo for the
art of WASSILY
KANDINSKY

Montréal

The mostly French-speaking city of Montréal is in east Canada, and is named after the Mount Royal peak at its center. It is famous for its food: bagels, poutine, and peanut butter, which was invented here in 1884! In summer, this cultural hub (and home of Le Cirque du Soleil) keeps everyone enteratined with comedy, jazz, and film festivals!

Can you find 5 MAPLE LEAVES?

Country: CANADA
Language: FRENCH
Population: 1.7 MILLION

Get green fingers at the MONTRÉAL BOTANICAL GARDEN'S Youth Garden

Watch an ICE HOCKEY MATCH at a local sports bar

Attend space camp at the COSMODÔME

Stock up on some sweet and sticky MAPLE SYRUP!

MAPLE Syrup

Bring a picnic to PARC DU MONT-ROYAL

Meet the mummies at the REDPATH MUSEUM

Go SLEDDING in the winter snow

Find Qumaluk's Walrus at the MONTRÉAL MUSEUM OF FINE ARTS

Treat yourself to a sweet BUTTER TART

Climb the 283 steps to ST. JOSEPH'S ORATORY

Have an adventure in SUMMIT WOODS

Meet the beavers at the BIODÔME

Take a boat along the ST. LAWRENCE RIVER

Visit the OLYMPIC STADIUM'S OBSERVATORY

Lark around in LAFONTAINE PARK

POLICE

Get into the swing of things at LA RONDE amusement park

Cycle around DOLPHIN LAKE

See the fireworks on ST. HELEN'S ISLAND

ST. LAWRENCE RIVER

Learn about the city's history at the NATIONAL LIBRARY AND ARCHIVES OF QUEBEC

Check your eco-footprint at the BIOSPHERE ENVIRONMENT MUSEUM

Enjoy some storytelling at the PLACE DES ARTS' junior Theater program

Catch the choir at NOTRE-DAME BASILICA

Go paddleboating off the OLD PORT OF MONTREAL

Try some of the world's best BAGELS

Try out a giant video game at the IMMERSION THEATER in the CENTRE DES SCIENCES

Bonjour

Check out the modern community of HABITAT 67

Find some peace and quiet inside the MARY, QUEEN OF THE WORLD CATHEDRAL

TORONTO

Toronto is the largest city in Canada and its most famous attraction is the CN Tower, which is North America's tallest tower. It is the country's cultural hub and there is a lot to do here. Ice hockey is the national sport, and doughnuts are the unofficial national food!

Can you find
5
HOT DOGS?

Country: CANADA
Language: ENGLISH
Population: 2.7 MILLION

Visit the ROYAL ONTARIO MUSEUM'S CENTRES OF DISCOVERY

Hunt for treasures at KENSINGTON MARKET

Milky Way

Have a pizza feast in LITTLE ITALY

Laugh out loud at the FESTIVAL OF CLOWNS

Gorge on the city's famous DOUGHNUTS!

Run off leash in HIGH PARK

Ride a glass elevator up the CN TOWER

Spot the seabirds from TORONTO HARBOUR

Try some authentic "street meat"—until 2009 HOT DOGS were the only street food allowed by law in Toronto!

HOT DOG MENU

Look out for GIBRALTAR POINT LIGHTHOUSE, one of the oldest buildings in the city

Run wild at RIVERDALE PARK

Explore the historic neighborhood of CABBAGETOWN

Meet the pigs and cows at the 19th-century-style RIVERDALE FARM

Stroll the boardwalk at THE BEACH

Go ice-skating at NATHAN PHILLIPS SQUARE

Spot Toronto's FLATIRON BUILDING, the GOODERHAM BUILDING

See the Stanley Cup at the HOCKEY HALL OF FAME

In summer, watch a film at the SAIL-IN CINEMA

Hello

Join a game of volleyball at CHERRY BEACH

Take a ferry to the TORONTO ISLANDS

Ride a giant swan at the CENTREVILLE AMUSEMENT PARK POND

LAKE ONTARIO

Play "explorers" along the LINCOLN PARK TRAILS

See a free musical story performance at LINCOLN PARK ZOO

Follow the Yellow Brick Road in OZ PARK

LINCOLN PARK

Visit the CHICAGO HISTORY MUSEUM

Chicago History Museum

Try your hand at baseball at the WICKER PARK pitch

Eat a foot-long HOT DOG!

Fly a Kite in the WINDY CITY

Make your own CHICAGO-STYLE PIZZAS

Catch a performance at the CHICAGO CHILDREN'S THEATRE

Listen to some CHICAGO BLUES

Rent KAYAKS on the river

Spot the PICASSO sculpture in the Chicago Loop

Climb to the SKY Ledge of the WILLIS TOWER for great views of the city!

CHICAGO

Sometimes called the Windy City, Chicago is home to the boogie-woogie, the Chicago blues, and Sue, the world's largest Tyrannosaurus rex! The Ferris wheel was also invented in Chicago—head here for sweeping views of the towering skyscrapers that make this city the metropolis of the American Midwest.

Can you find 5 AMERICAN FOOTBALLS?

Country: UNITED STATES OF AMERICA
Language: ENGLISH
Population: 2.7 MILLION

40

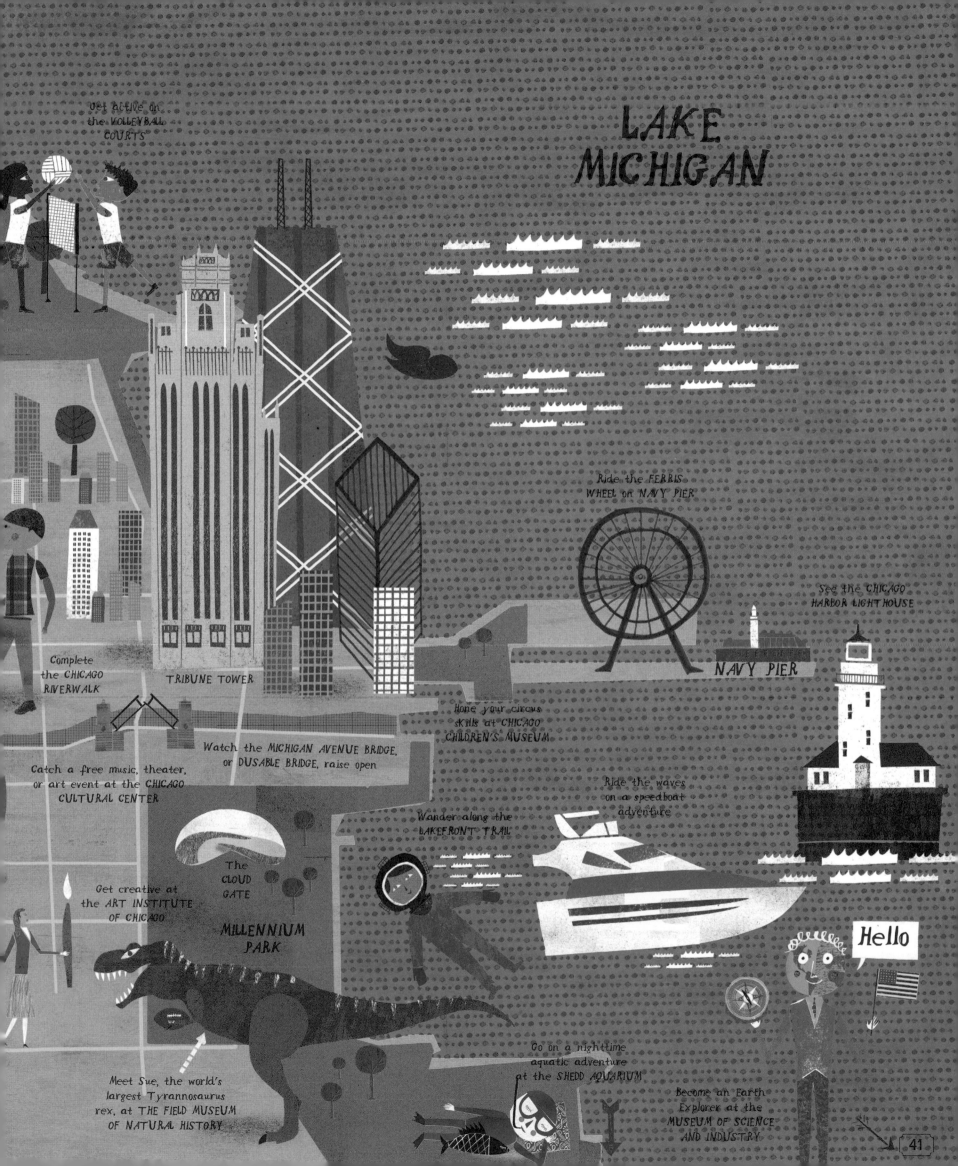

Get active on the VOLLEYBALL COURTS

LAKE MICHIGAN

Ride the FERRIS WHEEL on NAVY PIER

See the CHICAGO HARBOR LIGHTHOUSE

NAVY PIER

Complete the CHICAGO RIVERWALK

TRIBUNE TOWER

Hone your circus skills at CHICAGO CHILDREN'S MUSEUM

Watch the MICHIGAN AVENUE BRIDGE, or DUSABLE BRIDGE, raise open

Catch a free music, theater, or art event at the CHICAGO CULTURAL CENTER

Ride the waves on a speedboat adventure

Wander along the LAKEFRONT TRAIL

Get creative at the ART INSTITUTE OF CHICAGO

The CLOUD GATE

MILLENNIUM PARK

Hello

Meet Sue, the world's largest Tyrannosaurus rex, at THE FIELD MUSEUM OF NATURAL HISTORY

Go on a nighttime aquatic adventure at the SHEDD AQUARIUM

Become an Earth Explorer at the MUSEUM OF SCIENCE AND INDUSTRY

Wave from the crown of the
STATUE OF LIBERTY

N408TD

HUDSON RIVER

Hi there!

Get jazzy in the neighborhood of GREENWICH VILLAGE

Pencil in some time at the CHILDREN'S MUSEUM OF THE ARTS

Catch a street performance in WASHINGTON SQUARE PARK

Climb the spiderweb at PIER 25 HUDSON RIVER PARK

WALL STREET JOURNAL

Pick up your perfect patty at PAUL'S DA BURGER JOINT

Find pizza perfection in LITTLE ITALY

Be the top dog in TOMPKINS SQUARE PARK

See the historic ships at SOUTH STREET SEAPORT

ELLIS ISLAND

AMBROSE

BROOKLYN BRIDGE

Make a crossing on the STATEN ISLAND FERRY

Find your flavor at BROOKLYN ICE CREAM FACTORY

Ride Jane's Carousel in BROOKLYN BRIDGE PARK

Stock up on invisibility powder at the BROOKLYN SUPERHERO SUPPLY COMPANY

Spend a day in PROSPECT PARK

Plant yourself in BROOKLYN BOTANIC GARDEN

42

Hit a high note at the METROPOLITAN OPERA

Explore the mammoth AMERICAN MUSEUM OF NATURAL HISTORY

CENTRAL PARK

Watch a baseball game at the YANKEE STADIUM

Speed down the WEST SIDE HIGHWAY BIKE PATH

Walk like an Egyptian at the METROPOLITAN MUSEUM

Spot a snow leopard in CENTRAL PARK ZOO

Go gaga for art at the GUGGENHEIM MUSEUM

Make your mark at a MOMA workshop

Start your own toy story at FAO SCHWARZ

Explore the sleek, chic neighborhood of the UPPER EAST SIDE

MANHATTAN ISLAND

Lose your train of thought at GRAND CENTRAL TERMINAL

VEGETABLE SOUP

Stand and stare at the foot of the CHRYSLER BUILDING

EAST RIVER

EAST RIVER FERRY

Try one of New York's finest inventions at a HOT DOG CART

Go for a dip at the McCARREN PARK POOL

BROOKLYN

NEW YORK

New York, New York! This is the most populous city in America! Known alternately as the Big Apple and an urban jungle—either way, it's a hive of activity. Enjoy its iconic skyline of skyscrapers, eat a burger that's twice your size, and get lost in the sights and smells of the city.

Can you find 5 YELLOW TAXIS?

Country: UNITED STATES OF AMERICA
Language: ENGLISH
Population: 8.4 MILLION

San Francisco

This exciting city on America's West Coast is built on seven hills. Make a break for freedom on a trip to Alcatraz, hang with the hippies in the Haight, and cross the Golden Gate Bridge.

Can you find **5** SEA LIONS?

Country: UNITED STATES OF AMERICA
Language: ENGLISH
Population: 0.83 MILLION

Run through the rugged landscapes of GOLDEN GATE NATIONAL RECREATION AREA

Get crafty at the BAY AREA DISCOVERY MUSEUM

Cross the grand GOLDEN GATE BRIDGE

See the spectacular view from CRISSY FIELD, Presidio's "front door"

Hello

THE GOLDEN GATE

Stroll the sandy stretch of BAKER BEACH

Wander along the windswept shoreline of LANDS END park

Enter the oasis of GOLDEN GATE PARK

Meet Claude, the albino alligator at the CALIFORNIA ACADEMY OF SCIENCES

Follow the stepping stone paths inside the JAPANESE TEA GARDEN

Marvel at the magnificent spring magnolias in SAN FRANCISCO BOTANICAL GARDEN

Bury treasure on OCEAN BEACH

Make some friends at the Giraffe Barn Open House in SAN FRANCISCO ZOO

Take a ferry and a picnic to ANGEL ISLAND

Make a break for freedom in the infamous ALCATRAZ ISLAND AND PRISON

Board the historic ships at the MARITIME NATIONAL HISTORICAL PARK

FISHERMAN'S WHARF OF SAN FRANCISCO

Rent bikes and cycle along the seafront

Meet the sea lions at PIER 39

Follow your curiosty at the EXPLORATORIUM, MUSEUM OF SCIENCE, ART, AND HUMAN PERCEPTION

Pop into the PALACE OF FINE ARTS

Wind your way down the crooked LOMBARD ST.

Explore the old beatnik haunts and learn about ALLEN GINSBERG and JACK KEROUAC

Hear the cables sing in the streets at the CABLE CAR MUSEUM

Explore the YERBA BUENA CHILDREN'S GARDENS in the heart of the city's downtown cultural district

Visit the Painted Ladies at ALAMO SQUARE

Get hands-on in the CHILDREN'S CREATIVITY MUSEUM

Ride a Powell-Hyde open-air cable car from POWELL ST. TO FISHERMAN'S WHARF

Hang out with hippies in the HAIGHT-ASHBURY DISTRICT

Escape the bustle of the city at HAYES VALLEY FARM

Chill out with an ice cream in the MISSION DOLORES neighborhood

Play I Spy at the SQUARE OF THE THREE CULTURES

Don your dancing shoes for the mariachi bands at PLAZA GARIBALDI

Watch a traditional folklore ballet at the PALACIO DE BELLAS ARTES

Light a candle inside the sacred CATEDRAL METROPOLITANA

Put a trip to the ancient city TEOTIHUACAN at the top of your list!

Go to the giant government building of the NATIONAL PALACE

Munch on some MEXICAN MAIZE, or corn

Tap your foot to the folk music of the MARIACHI BANDS

Meet millions of migrating MONARCH BUTTERFLIES

Scoot along to the SKATEPARK

Try some tasty MAGUEY, a kind of cactus

MEXICO CITY

Mexico City, the capital of the country Mexico, is one of the biggest and most important cities in all of the Americas. Once the capital of the Aztec Empire, today it is celebrated for its colorful culture. This streets here are bursting with great food, museums, music, and murals—be sure not to miss the Frida Kahlo Museum or the mariachi bands!

Can you find 5 BLUE SKULLS?

Country: MEXICO
Language: SPANISH
Population: 9 MILLION

RIO DE JANEIRO

This vibrant city is bordered by white sand beaches, tropical forests, and majestic mountains. Each year it hosts the world's largest party, Carnival, but the city and landscape provide entertainment all year round.

Can you find **5** TANAGER BIRDS?

Country: BRAZIL
Language: PORTUGUESE
Population: 6.3 MILLION

Have lunch by the lake in QUINTA DA BOA VISTA

Join a jungle jeep SAFARI

Olá

Travel on the rack railway to the top of CORCOVADO MOUNTAIN

Walk to a waterfall in PARQUE NACIONAL DA TIJUCA

Spot a lot of OCELOTS

Wander around the public park PARQUE ENRIQUE LAGE

Discover a forest filled with DORMIDEIRA flowers

Spot a TOUCAN in the treetops

Take a bike trip around RODRIGO DE FREITAS LAGOON

Go stargazing at FUNDAÇÃO PLANETÁRIO DA CIDADE DO RIO DE JANEIRO

Have a party at the PLATAFORMA SAMBA SHOW

Learn about Carnival at the SAMBA MUSEUM

Hitch a ride on the SANTA TERESA TRAM

Visit the Mayan-inspired CATEDRAL METROPOLITANA

Tour the NATIONAL HISTORY MUSEUM

Let loose at the FUNDIÇÃO PROGRESSO THEATER

Watch fire-eaters and stilt-walkers on the WATERFRONT

Climb up to the statue of CHRIST THE REDEEMER

Drink coconut milk on the BEACH

Take a cable car up SUGARLOAF MOUNTAIN

Get creative with body paint at MUSEU DO ÍNDIO

Ride a zip wire across PARQUE DA CATACUMBA

Have a sandcastle competition on COPACABANA BEACH

Amble along AVENIDA ATLÂNTICA

Spend a lazy day on IPANEMA BEACH

Surf the waves on the southern point of COPACABANA BEACH

SOUTH ATLANTIC OCEAN

49

Go game, set, and match at the ARGENTINA TENNIS COURTS

Play in the water pools at PARQUE NORTE

Pet the Koi carp in the ornamental ponds of JARDÍN JAPONÉS

Feed the llamas at JARDÍN ZOOLÓGICO

Ride around the city in a HORSE-DRAWN CARRIAGE

Find the Buddhist Temple in the JAPANESE GARDENS

MUSEO NACIONAL DE BELLAS ARTES

Order a SUBMARINO and make your own hot chocolate

SUBMARINO

Try some of the famous ARGENTINIAN ICE CREAM

Roam around the tombs and elaborate mausoleums at the famous CEMENTERIO DE LA RECOLETA

Explore MUSEO DE LOS NIÑOS, the Children's Museum

Get a guided tour of the dinosaurs at the BERNARDINO RIVADAVIA NATURAL SCIENCE MUSEUM

Spot a TROPICAL PARULA

Hola

Relax by the pond at PARQUE CENTENARIO

BUENOS AIRES

Buenos Aires, home to famous "porteños" Eva Perón and football legend Diego Maradona, is the capital of Argentina. It is made up of 48 districts, called "barrios," and each one is a wonderful mix of European architecture and Argentinian culture. It is world-famous for its cafe culture, polo matches, and fiery tango dancing.

Can you find 5 LLAMAS?

Country: ARGENTINA
Language: SPANISH
Population: 3 MILLION

Take your chance to dance the TANGO

RIO DE LA PLATA

Tuck into a STEAK—one of the best you'll find in the world!

Play hide-and-seek in PARQUE THAYS

Explore the city by BIKE

See the OBELISK lit up at night

Inspect the must-see CATEDRAL METROPOLITANA

Cross the PUENTE DE LA MUJER

Escape the city in the RESERVA ECOLÓGICA COSTANERA SUR

Pop into the PALACIO DEL CONGRESO NACIONAL ARGENTINO, seat of the Argentine National Congress

See a show at the MUSEO ARGENTINO DEL TÍTERE puppet museum

Explore the weekend markets of FERIA DE SAN TELMO

Watch a match at LA BOMBONERA, the Boca Juniors soccer stadium

SOUTH ATLANTIC
OCEAN

Try out the
SPRINGBOK EXPERIENCE
RUGBY MUSEUM

Watch for whales
along the BANTRY BAY

Watch a game at
GREEN POINT STADIUM

See the spectacular
views from SIGNAL HILL,
or "LION'S RUMP"

Try a kind of syrup
doughnut called a
KOEKSISTER

Visit the IZIKO
PLANETARIUM'S
celestial theater

Try some local
spiced "BREDIE" STEW

Kayak your way
along CAMPS BAY

Wonder at the works of the
IZIKO SOUTH AFRICAN
NATIONAL GALLERY

Meet the baboons
at CAPE POINT

Watch the
fishing boats in
HOUT BAY HARBOUR

Ride a cable car to the
top of TABLE MOUNTAIN

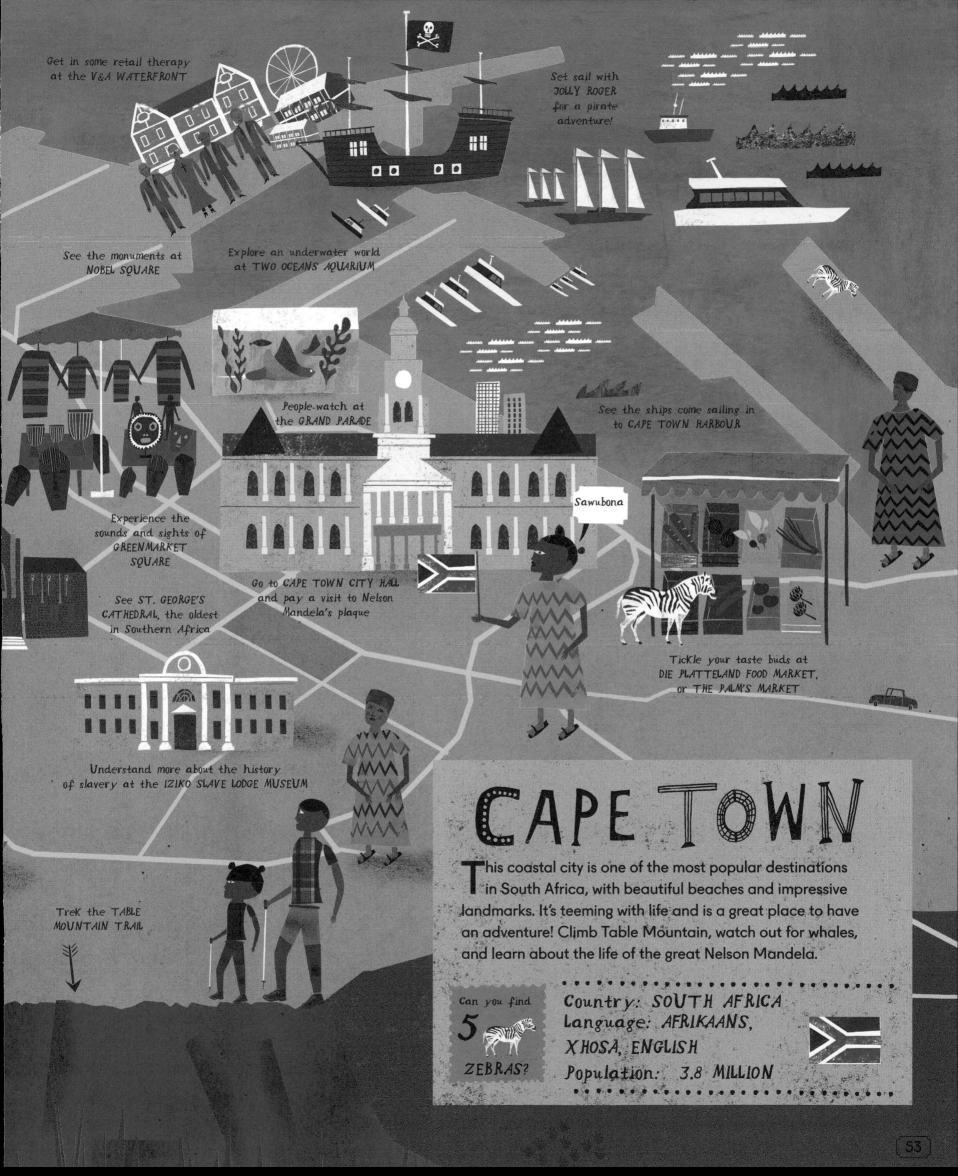

Get in some retail therapy at the V&A WATERFRONT

Set sail with JOLLY ROGER for a pirate adventure!

See the monuments at NOBEL SQUARE

Explore an underwater world at TWO OCEANS AQUARIUM

People-watch at the GRAND PARADE

See the ships come sailing in to CAPE TOWN HARBOUR

Experience the sounds and sights of GREENMARKET SQUARE

Sawubona

Go to CAPE TOWN CITY HALL and pay a visit to Nelson Mandela's plaque

See ST. GEORGE'S CATHEDRAL, the oldest in Southern Africa

Tickle your taste buds at DIE PLATTELAND FOOD MARKET, or THE PALM'S MARKET

Understand more about the history of slavery at the IZIKO SLAVE LODGE MUSEUM

Trek the TABLE MOUNTAIN TRAIL

CAPE TOWN

This coastal city is one of the most popular destinations in South Africa, with beautiful beaches and impressive landmarks. It's teeming with life and is a great place to have an adventure! Climb Table Mountain, watch out for whales, and learn about the life of the great Nelson Mandela.

Can you find 5 ZEBRAS?

Country: SOUTH AFRICA
Language: AFRIKAANS, XHOSA, ENGLISH
Population: 3.8 MILLION

ZHUJIANG RIVER ESTUARY

您好

Look out for a traditional DUK LING CHINESE SAILING BOAT

Ride the Ngong Ping cable car to PO LIN MONASTERY

Climb up to the foot of the gigantic TIAN TAN BUDDHA on Lantau Island

Hong Kong

This spellbinding city, both ancient and modern at the same time, is a treat for the senses with thousands of sights, sounds, and smells. Lose yourself in this dazzling city of towers, make a wish at the Lam Tsuen Wishing Trees, and take an adventure along the Dragon's Back trail.

Can you find **5** LUCKY DRAGONS

Country: CHINA
Language: CANTONESE, ENGLISH
Population: 7 MILLION

Jump in the water at TUNG WAN BEACH

Celebrate the CHEUNG CHAU BUN FESTIVAL

Make a wish and hope your dreams come true at the LAM TSUEN WISHING TREES

Discover the SIK SIK YUEN WONG TAI SIN TEMPLE, home to three religions

Get a glimpse of the past at the HONG KONG MUSEUM OF HISTORY

Watch the fishing boats off HONG KONG HARBOR

See the city light show from the TSIM SHA TSUI PROMENADE

Cruise on the famous STAR FERRY

Visit the FLAGSTAFF HOUSE MUSEUM OF TEA WARE, the oldest colonial residence in Hong Kong

Discover MAN MO TEMPLE, a calm oasis in the urban jungle

Ride to the top of the BANK OF CHINA TOWER

Breakfast on DIM SUM, thought by some to have inspired the idea of "brunch"!

Take a tram ride to VICTORIA PEAK, the highest point on Hong Kong Island

Hike the DRAGON'S BACK TRAIL—voted the best urban hiking trail in Asia

Have a picnic by WATERFALL BAY in Pok Fu Lam

Visit the OCEAN AMUSEMENT PARK

Spot pink dolphins on a DOLPHIN WATCH TOUR

Visit the fishing village on LAMMA ISLAND

Head to a JAPANESE TEA HOUSE for some Wagashi, traditional Japanese sweets

Lose yourself in the old town of YANAKA

今日は

Feel like a star singing KARAOKE

Practise the spring tradition of HANAMI with a picnic under the cherry blossom trees

Meet the pandas at UENO ZOO

See the city from a Tokyo HATO BUS TOUR

Take time out to take in the IMPERIAL PALACE AND GARDENS

Watch a bunraku puppet show at the NATIONAL THEATRE

See the monster fish at TSUKIJI, the world's largest fish market

Visit the magical MEIJI JINGU SHRINE

Get your dinner... from a VENDING MACHINE!

¥500 ¥500

¥500 ¥500

Make some feline friends at one of Toyko's famous CAT CAFES

See the illuminations of the TOKYO TOWER at night

Relax in THE PRINCE PARK

ASIMO

Walk underwater at the SHINAGAWA AQUARIUM

Explore the Sensō-ji temple in ASAKUSA

Climb the TOKYO SKYTREE, one of the world's tallest towers!

TOKYO

Tokyo is Japan's capital, where you'll find age-old traditions colliding with bright lights and super skylines. Find your fortune at the Sensō-ji temple, meet some real sumo wrestlers, and see the monster fish at the world's largest fish market!

Can you find TEAPOTS?

Country: JAPAN
Language: JAPANESE
Population: 9 MILLION

Grab your chopsticks and try some SUSHI

See the sumo wrestlers at the RYŌGOKU KOKUGIKAN SUMO HALL

Spot MOUNT FUJI from the top of the DIAMOND AND FLOWER FERRIS WHEEL

TOKYO PORT

Take a trip to TOKYO SEA LIFE PARK

Meet ASIMO the walking robot at MIRAIKAN, THE NATIONAL MUSEUM OF EMERGING SCIENCE AND INNOVATION

Visit some Korean Hanok houses in BUKCHON

Time-travel with THE NATIONAL FOLK MUSEUM OF KOREA

Explore the grounds of the old GYEONGBOKGUNG PALACE

Visit the JOGYESA Buddhist Temple

See what's happening at the GLOBAL CULTURE AND TOURISM CENTER

Pass through the NAMDAEMUN GATE, one of the "Eight Gates" in the Fortress Wall of Seoul

Ride a cable car to the top of MOUNT NAMSAN

See some traditional TAEKKYEON MARTIAL ARTS

Take the SEOUL CITY TOUR BUS

See the skyscrapers in DONGJA-DONG

N. Seoul Tower

Celebrate the spring cherry blossom on YEOUISEO-RO STREET

Enjoy some tasty KIMCHI

Explore the WAR MEMORIAL OF KOREA, filled with memorabilia and military equipment

Watch the street performers during the YEOUIDO SPRING FLOWER FESTIVAL

HAN RIVER

SEOUL

Check out CHANGDEOKGUNG PALACE, one of the "Five Grand Palaces"

Discover the "Secret Garden" at the CHANGDEOKGUNG PALACE

Cross the stepping stones of the CHEONGGYECHEON STREAM

Seoul, officially known as Seoul Special City, is the rapidly growing capital of South Korea. This city is famous for its modern technology, and there is something happening, day or night—step inside a teahouse or a temple for some peace and quiet, or check out its buzzing streets and markets if you're looking for action!

Can you find 5 FANS?

Country: KOREA
Language: KOREAN
Population: 10 MILLION

Try some sweet pumpkin rice cake in a traditional KOREAN TEAHOUSE

Feed the deer in SEOUL FOREST

Explore the ginormous NAMSAN PARK

Make a trip to the SEOUL CHILDREN'S MUSEUM

안녕하세요

Run around HANGANG CITIZENS' PARK

Feast on BIBIMBAP!

Enjoy a dance performance at the NATIONAL GUGAK CENTER

See the thousands of lanterns at the BONGEUNSA TEMPLE!

See the water fountain dance at the SEOUL ARTS CENTER

Walk with dinosaurs at the GWACHEON NATIONAL SCIENCE MUSEUM

59

ARABIAN
SEA

See the SACRED COWS
that roam the streets

See a performance at
the PRITHVI THEATRE
for children

Ride the toy train at the
RAJESH KHANNA GARDEN

Take a RICKSHAW
ride through the
city's streets

Learn about
the great
MAHATMA GANDHI

Enjoy a bit of
people-watching in
MAHIM NATURE PARK

Admire the HAJI ALI
DARGAH MOSQUE

Honor the god Ganesh with
a visit to the SHREE SIDDHIVINAYAK
GANAPATI MANDIR

Spot the flamingos
on the SEWRI
MUDFLATS between
November and March

Go stargazing at the
NEHRU PLANETARIUM

Take a trip to
the temple of
MAHALAKSHMI

Check out the
chimes of the
RAJABAI
CLOCK TOWER

Pass through the
impressive GATEWAY
OF INDIA

Be treated like
royalty in the TAJ
MAHAL PALACE HOTEL

MUMBAI

More people live in this vibrant metropolis than any other city in India. Known for its fantastic food and colorful culture, its busy streets have a surprise at every turn!

Can you find **5** SACRED COWS?

Country: INDIA
Language: GUJARATI, HINDI, MARATHI
Population: 12 MILLION

Snack on samosas as you stroll through SANJAY GANDHI NATIONAL PARK

Explore the amazing KANHERI CAVES

Celebrate DIWALI, the autumnal Hindu festival of lights

Dance along to a BOLLYWOOD MOVIE

Try the real BOMBAY MIX from a street vendor

Explore the rock temples of ELEPHANTA ISLAND

Take a ferry to Elephanta Island

हॅलो

61

PARRAMATTA
RIVER

Have a roller coaster of
a day at LUNA PARK

LUNA PARK

SYDNEY
HARBOUR
BRIDGE

Learn some circus skills at the
SYDNEY OLYMPIC PARK AQUATIC CENTRE

Enjoy a picnic
on OBSERVATORY HILL

Watch the boats
in SYDNEY HARBOUR

Learn the ropes at
URBAN JUNGLE
ADVENTURE PARK

Get spooked
on a GHOST
TOUR

Have an
encounter with
a Koala at
WILD LIFE,
SYDNEY ZOO

Get the top
spot in the
SYDNEY
TOWER EYE

Check out
the view from
WATERFRONT
PARK

Play on the gian
chess set in
NAGOYA GARDENS

Go fishing at the
SYDNEY FISH MARKET... the
third largest in the world!

Shop till you drop
in the QUEEN
VICTORIA BUILDING

Meet Australia's most
deadly animals in the
AUSTRALIA MUSEUM

Join the
debate at
SYDNEY
TOWN HALL

Power up your imagination at
the POWERHOUSE MUSEUM

Meet a mummy at
the NICHOLSON
MUSEUM

Learn to surf on MANLY BEACH

Watch for whales from the FAIRFAX WALKING TRACK

See some friendly faces at TARONGA ZOO

G'day

Catch a concert at the SYDNEY OPERA HOUSE

Sit in MRS. MACQUARIE'S CHAIR at Sydney Harbour

Set sail for SHARK ISLAND

See a film at the ST. GEORGE OPEN-AIR CINEMA

Take a trip to the SYDNEY TROPICAL CENTRE

Discover a tropical paradise at the ROYAL BOTANIC GARDENS

Hit someone for six at SYDNEY CRICKET GROUND

Get a bird's-eye view of the city in a HOT AIR BALLOON

SYDNEY

Sydney is an exciting, multicultural city that attracts people from all over the world. It's close to great sandy beaches and is always bustling with activity. Learn to surf, watch out for whales, and meet some of Australia's most deadly animals.

Can you find **5** KOALA BEARS?

Country: AUSTRALIA
Language: ENGLISH
Population: 4.2 MILLION

Go for the ride of your life in CENTENNIAL PARK

To Tibor and Arthur

Wide Eyed Editions
www.wideeyededitions.com

City Atlas © Aurum Press Ltd 2015
Illustrations copyright © Martin Haake 2015

Written by Georgia Cherry

First published in the United States in 2015 by Wide Eyed Editions
an imprint of Quarto Inc.,
276 Fifth Avenue, Suite 206, New York, NY 10001.
www.wideeyededitions.com

LOC number pending

ISBN 978-1-84780-701-4

The illustrations were created digitally
Set in Fugue, Haake bold 04

Designed by Andrew Watson
Edited by Jenny Broom
Published by Rachel Williams

Printed in Dongguan, Guangdong, China

1 3 5 7 9 8 6 4 2